Oswald's Book of Hours

Oswald's Book of Hours
Steve Ely

Published 2013 by
Smokestack Books
PO Box 408, Middlesbrough TS5 6WA
e-mail: info@smokestack-books.co.uk
www.smokestack-books.co.uk

Oswald's Book of Hours
Cover image: from Gaston Phébus, *Le Livre de Chasse*
Author photo: Jane Ely

Printed by Martins the Printers
EPW Print & Design Ltd

ISBN 978-0-9571722-3-4

Smokestack Books is
represented by Inpress Ltd
www.inpressbooks.co.uk

'Some day we shall get up before the dawn
And find our ancient hounds before the door,
And wide-awake know that the hunt is on;'

W.B. Yeats, *Hound Voice*

Contents

Kalendarium

Edward, Duke of York, the Master of Game

… we rose at daybreak on the feast of the holy cross
and rode to the chace, where we breakfasted in our tents,
apples and white bread and frankish grape-wine,
fumes curling from the jar like dawn-mist rising over the stank,
scarlet as the eastern sky, as the boar's-blood smeared
on beardless cheeks by the index and middle fingers
of aethelfrith, my father, who was pagan and barbarian
and took me to hunt the eofor in the water-waste of haethfelt,
where i leapt from my mount in the birch-scrub
by the turbary to drive home the barbed iron
in a tumult of pigshriek, yelping greyhounds, alauntes snarling,
mallard and hernshaw, panicking aloft –
my father smiling, the roars and backslaps
of war-gloried men – i tell you, it is no synne …

… the ninth hour of michaelmas
and my hard ridden heat as hot as the heat of the hart
at abbay under the crag at maelmin, slavered in the sweat
of its running, snorting snot and throwing its head
at the coupled curs and mastiffs straining at their cords
with blue lips curled and white teeth bared,
men with bows and haronblasts, pinning it to its death.
in the cloudless blue an eagle is over the crag,
launching the corbyn skyward.
i prayed for the intercession of the great prince of angels
and thanked god for his bounty, before striding
through the heather with sword-edge bared
and great anxiety in my heart, for is it not said,
'after the boar the leech, after the hart the bier'?
the slipped dogges leapt forward and the hart
crotyed great fumes and lurched to meet them
tossing curs aloft and stamping them under,
great biting of mastiffs yet pulling him down.

my sword bit deep and touched his heart.
we made the curee on his own hide
there under the crag at maelmin, and man and dogge
had of his flesh their share and even the corbyn
had their bone. and we rode to our tents
with much laughter and shouting, the hounds
smiling and leaping and wagging their tails
and all had surfeit of joy, as did david and samson
and nimrod before them and thus it is no sinne …

… in advent i have no hunting, for advent
is a little lent wherefore christian men should abstain
and prepare for the coming of haeland the christ.
this i learned this from acha, my mother, and columba
the abbot of hii. in this tyme i repaireth oft to my kennels
for i have much love for my various hounds and curs
in their shapes and making and reason
and obedience, for there is none of god's creatures
that loveth to do man's will as do dogges.
and i have small curs named terriers
that go under the earth to drive out conies and the gray;
lymers that scenteth harts in their harbours,
and all other game that giveth good nose;
alauntes of the chase and fleet greyhounds
that runneth down wolf and the hare;
mastiffs and burly curs that slashed by tusk and gored by horn
will grip the savage eofor and hold the hart at bay.
and dogges have great joy in the company of men,
coming grinning and whining with kissing
and licking, much leaping and wagging of tail.
and men have great joy in the company of dogges
feeding trenchers from the table,
stroking and caressing them, repeating their names
and affirming they are good, which pleaseth them much.
for dogges are brave and loyal and true
and will kill gladly and die in the service of their masters.
and it is a great and glorious thing to see dogges at the chase,
encoupled with hunting men, each in fulfilment of his nature,
which god himself has pleased to shape
and thus can be no synne …

… on the feast of stephen we set out from cambodunum
in snow very deep like goose feathers strewn
in the barn where maidens plucketh.
we sought whatever we might find in that condition
and did start many foxes from the woods
around the vills, where they lurketh in the winter
to seize fowls, small beestys and the lambs of sheep.
slowed by their red bellies dragging in the snow,
my long-legged alauntes ran them down
and slew them by the throat, for which the villeins had great joy
and praised us with hallooing and cheering,
wherefore i say it is no sin. the pelts were thick
as summer sedge and the tanners had their profit.
but the flesh of fox is not fit for men
and ruinous to the temper of dogges.
so we left the meat for scavenging corbyn,
ligged in reddening snow. crouch-cloaked
on our iron-spurred steeds, snotted with ice
and steaming like the byre, we galloped to hall,
eager for feasting …

… south of eoforwic, the derwent hath mightily flooded
and the hare is this winter driven to the frost-hard wold.
the hare has no season, yet after candlemas,
some say she cannot be taken, for then she cometh
into her heat and is quick with leverets.
yet i affirm the hare may farrow in any month
and thus has no season and may be taken at any time
by strength of hounds. for ice-bit hours we rode the wold,
flushing nought but bustards. then, with daylight closing to vespers,
the cry went up and we flushed a solitary hare.
the houndes uncoupled, she ran them in great circles, as is her wont,
across field and common, into copses and bankings,
the houndes giving mouth and making good gallop,
but gaining little ground, until, her breath beginning to fail
and perceiving her death, she put back her ears
and raced downhill to the ice-bound valley,
seeing there a stratagem to save her life.

whereupon i slipped the greyhounds,
which took her, with much tumbling and sliding,
on the ice by the open river, amidst tumult of whoopers
and blizzarding wigeon, trumpeting and whistling,
each after the manner of their kind.
the meat i gave to a poor man of those parts,
adding virtue to virtue, for in none of these is sinn ...

... that st mark's morning in the forest at heavenfelt
the littel birdis did sing in company
like counterpoint of monks in choir, the throstle
and the blackbird and the distant cucu.
and through the green-leaved beech-boughs,
the warm sonne speared to the bluebelled floor
like spokes from a fiery wheel. and smoke was rising
over the forest, from the log-fire roasting the spitted-bear
we surprised by the beck as he drinketh and did take with dogges
and the thrusts of many spears. and that morn
i had much pleasure of birdsong and the daffodil sonne-light
and the leafs and croppes of lententime,
not merely in the chasce of the bear; for in these small things
is for the hunter great joy and praising of the lord.
but some men that were with us put his head
and arms on poles and quoth, 'behold cadwallon, bear
of the britons'. but them i berated; for though it
be no synne to take a bear in the forest of heaven,
it maketh cruell a man to desport with his body
and insolent also to make of that beast a king,
dead and in hell though that pagan king may be ...

... the feast of st john cometh three days after
the fires of midsummer and on that day begins
the season for hart and buck and hind
and some say endeth that of the river-fitch named otter,
which i nevertheless say is vermin and folly,
thus having no season, as the foulmart, ermine and miniver.
and in my forest at gefrin we encountered low-born men
of our people, with bows and spears and hairy curs
with broad feet and well-clawed toes, which hackled
and growled and spoiled to fight with our couples,
which nevertheless gave shout and good nose and led us
to the carcass of the hind concealed in bracken.

having kneeled the churls at sword-edge,
i demanded they account for their arrogance
in stealing a deer from the forest of oswald their king.
they bowed their heads and none dare speak,
until the boldest saieth, 'sir, it is no synne for an englisc-manne
to take a deer from his own landis forest.'
and i could not fault him ...

Godspel

'Siþþan eastan hider
Engle & Seaxe up becoman,
ofer brad brimu Brytene sohtan,
wlance wigsmiþas, Weealas ofercoman,
eorlas arhwate eard begeatan.'

The Battle of Brunanburh

Incipit euangelium secundum Aethelstan Rex

1. How shall I advise an English king who already is a Saint? And how shall I not reflect that his canonical destiny should also have been mine; for did I not fight for the godspelle angyn Haelendes Criste, against the rage of heathen men? 2. Did I not drive from our borders the pagan Norse, heretic Welsh and traitors of Strathclyde, for which am lauded in the song? 3. And did I not gather the bones of saints, holy blood and holy thorn, establish chapel and chantry for munuc and nunne? 4. I used to curse God that I died in my sleep at Malmesbury and not on the field at Brunanburh, at the edge of pagan Guthfrith's sword; Papa Leo and Biscop Wulfhelm would have confirmed my cult within the year. 5. The Confessor still rankles with me; no English king, but a cringing stooge, hostage of the Bastard. His saintliness was fear and lack of virility; 6. The kingdom was Godwine's, rihtcynnes Englisc, father, and Harald, his son. 7. But enough of this prattle; to business. My counsel is Alfred's; 8. Fight for your people and your borders. Venerate your land. Grow your people in the ways of our rice; nuture them in the church. 9. Love God with all your heart and your neighbour as yourself. 10. Distrust the British. Show strength to stay the Scots. Bring Danes and those pagans willing to convert into the Angelfolc; but not others. 11. Take to the seas, make pilgrimage: Rome, Jerusalem, Constantinople, Kiev of Rus and saracen Zanzibar. 12. Plant your dead around the belltower in the green turf of the graveyard: remember them, venerate their memory and their deeds.

Incipit euangelium secundum Wat Tyler

1. Three things: firstly, and no offence; never trust a King. That was our downfall, the idiotic peasant conceit that a divine right tyrant propped up by a cabal of mammonite murderers could ever rule with the interests of his people at heart. 'King Richard and the true commons' my arse: 2. We frittered our rage on his circle, Gaunt and Sudbury, Walworth and Hales, named them hoodwinkers and deceivers, drippers of poison into the sainted royal ears; 3. But he was always one of them: if not of their class, of their interest; a purpled pisser into their plutocrat pisspot. 4. Secondly, when the kingdom is restless like the turbulent North Sea, ride the tumult of the people like a spratoon on the storm-tide; knowing when to paddle and when to spear, when to launch aloft in defiance of the breakers, where to find flat water for rest and respite before braving the squall again. 5. The chance came at Mile End; I should have slaughtered them all and stuck the boy's head on a pole; but, already light-headed on the revell, we allowed our egos to be flattered and fell for the kid-King's flim-flam. 6. He turned the rebellion, sent us settling scores and butchering flemings: 7. Divert, divide - and rule. And while we cavorted in our world upside down, his apple-cheeked majesty breathed counter-revolution with Walworth. 8. Which brings me to the third thing: let not the assurance of even a thirty thousand strong militia serve to turn your head or cause you to drop your guard. 9. Yeasted on success, my arrogance blinded

me to the masters' malice and my own vulnerability and I swaggered before them like a drunken churl. I paid with my life and the jubilee of the commons. 10. And yet there is a fourth thing: pray for the intercession of Ball: 11. His spirit is the strength of England, for he will fire the fieldfolk and seek to destroy those who live on their labour without themselves working: 12. Baron and banker, lawyer and lord, cleric and king. 13. From Eden were all men created alike, according to God's will and in His image; and the bondage of the many comes from the arrogance and grasping of the few: 14. Which is murder and breaking of brotherhood, the brand of Cain. 15. Sainted King Oswald, heed well my lesson. When your moment arrives, seize it: lead the fyrd of your people to palace of Westminster and hesitate not to treat it with fire; 16. And doubt not that your people, should you ever oppress them or lead them astray, will turn upon your Northumbrian tower, with springole and trebuchet, block, scaffold and hatchet.

Incipit euangelium secundum Robert Aske

1. You're alright asking me. All I wanted was the quiet life, then a mob turned up on my doorstep and before I knew it, I was at the gates of Danum flying the banner of the Five Wounds of Christ: 2. Whereupon my nerve failed and I listened to the King, naively choosing to trust his words rather than the forty thousand truehearts of my peoples' militia, their pikes and cannon and murderous intent. 3. Within a year, I was dangling headless from the walls of York Castle and the looting of our church, the destruction of our religion and the extirpation of our way of life continued with rapacity. 4. I was one of *them*, almost: knight's son, barrister, resident at the Inns of Court, descendent of the Cliffords, cousin to the Queen. It did me no good. 5. I always preferred to be at home at the manor in Aughton. On winter afternoons I'd lean on the wall of All Saints churchyard and look out over the fowl-snidered ings, pewits and plovers tumbling from the skies, skeining greylags, the whistling wingbeats of whoopers. 6. I'd watch the Wheldrake fowlers, setting their punts out over the waters, loaded with nets and baskets and nooses, mallard and pintail erupting before them; then floating back at eventide, loaded with ducks and brindled bitterns they'd bring daily to our kitchen. 7. In spring I'd watch the white owl haunting the twilight floodbank, drifting over the sheep like a tear of ectoplasm, crakes creaking from the ditches like the unquiet ghosts of Deira.

8. I long for it now, even from paradise: snipe whirring and whinnying over the lenten valley, the clamour of curlews, the thundering heaven of larks. 9. It was all I wanted: to live in my land and praise God in his seasons. 10. The white owl roosted in the rafters of the All Saints lych gate. As we entered for mass, we'd step in its coughed-up turds, the luck of St. Peter. 11. He stole our gold, our plate, our vestments of silk, our statues, saints and feasts. 12. Our way of life reduced to jobs. Religion reduced to propositions. Where once was meaning, now is only truth. 13. I should've followed the swords right through to Tyburn and made him kick at the end of a rope – *sic semper tyrannis*. The King is to serve the people, not the people to serve the King.

Incipit euangelium secundum Scouse McLaughlin

1. Death has changed me; I'm a lot calmer, mellow even. I've got a little garden, I go to mass every day: 2. You have regrets, you're bound to; everyone has. I'm sorry I blooded my son in that sheep, for the ears in my webbing, for not being the world's best husband: probably. 3. I was a shithead in barracks as well. I made a point of it, to let everyone know I was someone who couldn't be fucked with, to piss off the brass. 4. But I'll be honest with you; I can't say for certain I wouldn't get up to the same shit again. 5. Pay no attention to the middle classes, their self-serving dinner-party morality; *if they didn't want to die, they shouldn't have joined the army/all that trouble for a bunch of sheep farmers/two bald men fighting over a comb.* 6. They've no idea where they've come from, the spilled blood and sacrifice it's taken to get them to a place where they can reduce their carbon footprint over rocket and parmigiana and twitter on their iPhones insulated from the terror of the world. 7. I saw my friends cut to pieces around me. The ruperts were all croaked. There was nothing to do but take charge, so I did. 8. I rallied the lads. We ran up the hill into .50 calibre machine gun fire, bayoneting spics and getting our arms and legs blown off. I harvested their ears, like they did in 'nam. My idea was to make a necklace. It seemed like a lark at the time. 9. I carried wounded off the mountain through a minefield, ducking mortars and bullets with a sucking wound

so wide, you could reach in and grab my kidneys.   10. Then the shell hit: Goodnight Vienna. They screwed me out of my posthumous VC on account of the lugs, but God knows his own.   11. Remember what Wellington said on the eve of Waterloo: *I don't know the effect these men will have on the enemy, but by God they frighten me.*   12. And that's about the shape of it: plucky Tommy Atkins, (Gawd bless 'im) vs Booze Britain and the Inter City Firm. 13. It's like they say up here; *Daemon est Deus inversus.* Two sides of the same coin: you can't have one without the other. 14. And the next time the shit hits the fan, who you gonna call? The Independent? The Groucho Club? Alderley-fucking-Edge?   15. Oswald, King and Saint, I know one thing and one thing only: the rabble is the blood-pulse of England. Never forget it.

Prayers to the Virgin

Obsecro te

'If I had a hundred bodies I would suffer them all to be
torn into pieces rather than recant.'

Thomas Haukes, 9 June 1555, the day of his burning
at the hands of Queen Mary's men

Obsecro te regina Maria,
although I affirm my denial
of the Real Presence and reject once more
the Supremacy of the Pope, suffer me
yet to live; for shall not the lion lie down
with the lamb, Sudbury break bread with Ball?
Then should a sister reconcile with her brother
in the faith. Catkins break from quickening willow,
and spring's green titmice dart and cheep;
conies creep under doilied blackthorns
and from the kingcup-meadow, the hot fitch prowls;
blood rises with the sun that on my springtime smiles:
I was not born for death, for the faggots
and flames of Spain, but England's verdant Word.
Lady, the people will be turbulent
in tongue and in tract, the virtue and virility
of the race; wisdom, therefore, is to suffer
dissent and no ways to suppress. Let a table
be prepared beneath the blossoming crab-tree
and there come together your querulous breed,
to commune in beer and loaves of barley:
fyrd-food, the bread of our fathers.

O intemerata

'Forsake Anne Boleyn and take back your wife
Catherine... if you neglect this, you shall die the
death of a villain, and Mary, the daughter
of Catherine, shall wear your crown'.

Elizabeth Barton, the 'Nun of Kent', prophesying
to King Henry VIII in 1532, two years before he
ordered her burnt

O intemerata et virgo Maria,
now mottled like a throstle's breast
or the coat of a wall-eyed Romney sheep-dog.
Twice-sullied: by Spain's rotten sperm,
begetter of gut-ghosts and flatulence only,
yeasting your womb with the crown-prince of farts;
and divine right's Cain-brand, the red-merle rash
of poxy guilt congenital from your sire.
He withered you to hate with his scandal
and dismissal, hardening your heart
against the English people, turning your head
to the Alcazar and to Rome. You wore
his crown indeed, ever your father's daughter;
for Kings and Queens will burn: Tyburn's stake,
the pyres of purgatory – the incendiary torches
of the fishwives of Kent, shrieking through the halls
of Hampton Court Palace.

Hours of the Virgin

'...the night is black as pitch, the wind has risen
and the rain is hitting you in the face like shot.
Get moving, for this is your night.'

Frank Sheardown, *The Working Longdog*

Matins: Annunciation

Force eight from Lundy and the Irish Sea
in the dark moon of the solstice.
Alarmed awake at midnight, sleet slashing
across the window glass, blurring the street-lit world.
Packing the van in drenched Jack Pyke:
Lazerlight lamp-kit, slip-leads, dogs.
The long drive east to the ditch-cut flatlands.
Sleet strafing down. Wind howling in the hawthorns.
Shivering long-dogs, ears erect. The thousand foot
halogen beam. Green-eyes in hedge-bottoms.
Transfixed conies. Dogs running down the beam.
Conies dangling in the Deben double V.
Back to the van. Bag the necked and bladdered conies.
Towel and box the dogs. Peel off the drenched Jack Pyke.
The cold drive home in the dark moon of the solstice,
sleet slurring the view through the wiping-windscreen,
blurring the headlamped world.

Lauds: Visitation

Before the dogs are walked and wittled
is morning prayer: antiphons, psalms,
the Glory Be. Holy cripple, my office book
limps my bad faith through. Then the bridlepath
to Clayton in may-flower dawn, thrushes pealing
from the hedgerows like the clamour of church bells
on Sunday morning. My bobbery pack before me;
Plummers and whippets, Hancock lurchers,
flushing partridge from the bracken,
sending rabbit-kits scuttling earthward.
A scribbler's nest in broken gorse. A stoat
moustached with a shrew. A hill-crest ridged
in haloed Friesians, filing to first milking.
And striding over the stile in mutton-chop sideburns,
snared leveret bulging under his suit-coat,
from his fist a sockful of pheasant eggs
dangling; Lol Gifford, the keeper's bane
from the top of our street, greeting with a grin
and a *nah then lad*, making a fuss of the dogs.

Prime: Nativity

She whelped in the front room in a basket
by the hearth. The telly was on in the corner,
Good Morning Sports Fans. The lad flipped
it to SpongeBob, then went do his papers.
She'd done by the time he was back. Three dogs,
five bitches; blues and blacks, a fawn & brindle.
Sire, Lord of the Night from Mike Brown in Bridgend,
killed the week he covered her; breaking his neck
on a scarp at Torpantau, going hell for leather
for a hare. The black dog was runty,
kept falling off the tit. I gave it the weekend,
before drowning it in the sink. We made sure
she ate well, to keep her condition:
cottage cheese with powdered calcium,
the pluck of a rabbit, beef brisket diced small.
She was a good mother, barely leaving the basket
for the first three weeks, licking and cleaning,
giving good suck. Lads in flat caps
and Jack Pyke camo came calling.   At five weeks
they were spoken for, at ten, all gone,
bar the fawn and brindle boy, who we kept
for our own use, and who was dead in eighteen months,
ripping out his guts on dusk-blurred barbed-wire
going hell for leather for a hare.

Tierce: Annunciation to the Shepherds

No doubt some do-gooder ran breathless
to the farmer's door and knocked him out of bed:
somebody's had one of your sheep. I should have
fleece-wrapped the grallochs and stashed them
under a bush, instead of leaving them in the lay-by
for circling kites to announce to all and sundry.
I was showing off to the crows,
determined to show them what green-eyed means.
Nine in the morning, pissed out of our heads
from the all night lock-in. What was I thinking?
But I'd done it all my life, rabbits, hares,
deer and what have you; why not a sheep?
Fuck the farmers. So I pulled over
at the turning place, ran one down in the heather
and cut its throat with my Fairburn-Sykes.
Allahu akbhar. Anyway, the farmer called the bizzies,
and they made their enquiries, out there
on the Beacons having fuck all better to do,
apparently: turns out some nosey gwilum
had seen my weaving Hilux and made a note
of the plate. They found the carcass
hanging in the shower. Four hundred
plus costs, three months detention, suspended.
A six month tour in Helmand. Sheep coming
out of your arse over there.

Sext: Adoration of the Magi

August noon, seventy-nine. Short-cutting
from the res through waist-high barley,
going home for egg and chips.
I was singing Showaddywaddy, for no
particular reason; *re-member, re-re-remember,*
re-member, re-re-remember, re-member,
re-re-remember... then! The long mile home,
socks snagging in goose-grass, sun hitting like a plank
through my T-shirt's thin cotton, the straps
of my fishing box and shouldered rod,
rubbing my clavicles raw: *re-member, re-re-remember*
re-member, re-re-remember – THEN! crouched before me,
frozen massive in its form, the Grandad Hare,
staring me backwards with geoluread
terrified eyes. At Easter we'd flushed him
from Thyssen's field and lost him over the Green Hills;
last summer, we harried him from Frickley
to Burntwood, before cornering him on the Common,
where Trampus tripped and bowled him over,
then lost his sight in East Haigh's scrub. Now, frozen
in the moment, eye-to-eye once more. The barley shook
and he vanished, rippling the crop like wind,
fleeing straight into the mouths of Chris Slatter's
serendipitous deerhound-lurchers,
taking their morning constitutional,
which swerving and striking, coursed him tight
to the Carr Lane tunnel, nailing him in the lupin field
behind Pat Nicholson's house: where we gathered
and marvelled, bikes and fishing tackle dumped
where we dropped them, at the bloody corpse
of the ancient lepus, 'big as a labrador',
and the grinning gazehounds that finally
brought him down.

None: Presentation in the Temple

Dappled shade of Kirkby churchyard,
Whitsun, seventy-six. Beyond the walls,
sky cloudless brilliant blue; big sun burning down.
Bucolic cool within; turtles purring
from the breathing limes, swallows and martins
flicking between the graves, polyphon blackbird
and thrush. Bored. Tarzan off the wall
on the branches of the weeping ash.
Zipping unripe cherries at cars. Hide and seek.
Interlude to Blezzards, a can of Cresta
and a packet of Chuckles, then up to Tosh Larkin's
for his polecat and nets, some desultory ferreting
in the grounds of Northfield School. Too hot.
We bagged a brace and quit. Tosh legged them
through his snake-belt and we walked home
past the churchyard with them dangling from his waist.
Johnny Bradley was in there, commando crawling
between the graves, stalking blackies with his catty.
He called us over and offered a trade;
a rabbit for all his birds; and pulling back fronds
of camouflage burdock, revealed his dump
of feathery corpses, warm to the touch,
black eyeballs yet to dry; blackbirds and thrushes,
unbelievable swallows and martins -
a pair of crumpled turtle doves
in the suddenly silent graveyard.

Vespers: Massacre of the Innocents

Slipping into Pump Wood with the failing sun;
Parson Jack, lurcher, a risky .410.
No plan in particular – partridge, pheasant,
rabbit or hare – something for the pot.
Then they put up a buck from the rhododendrons
and ran it into the open cowfield.
Bellowing Holsteins, stamping and raging,
Parson and lurcher, giving loud tongue.
Not good. Raised voices in the stockyard,
farm dogs barking, a diesel engine coughing into life.
Brief silence, the distant Parson sounding;
then the blood-freezing *bok* of an angry twelve bore.
The Parson came whimpering back.
He led me through the oxlips to her body
by the five bar gate. Her ribcage was shattered.
Each dying breath belched blood. Somewhere in the blur
angry voices were gaining. Knuckles bleeding white
on the shotgun stock – *O God, come to our aid,*
O Lord make haste to help us.

Compline: Coronation of the Virgin

Blue-merle bitch; five-eighths greyhound, quarter collie,
one eighth bull. All legal quarry, and then some:
rabbit, walked-up or lamped; thirty
in one night at Boston last year, ten or twelve
routine. Fox, over fell or on flatland:
no contest. Muntjac and roe, a red deer once
at Thorne; she dragged it down by the throat
like a wolf. Unbeatable on hare.
Six on the stubbles at Swinefleet last August,
five the same week at Wharram in the Wolds.
Turn, trip, strike. Turn, trip, strike. She just keeps going.
Six weeks in pup, she nailed one on the common
and brought it back to hand. Stamina, speed,
intelligence and keenness to kill.
Nine she whelped, four dogs, five bitches.
Spoken for already, five hundred for the boys,
Seven fifty for the girls. Fieldhammer Lurchers,
it says on the website. No time-wasters.
I walked her round the block last night,
to empty her bowels. She pulled a cat
from under a car and broke it in half.
I threw it on the 638 as roadkill,
and hoped we'd gone unseen. She settled down
with her litter and watched me intently,
dicing tripes and ox-hearts at the kitchen table.
Outside, wind got up from nowhere
and rain came down in sheets, rattling
the darkened windows. Moon snuffed out by clouds.
May the Lord grant us a quiet night and a perfect end.

Hours of the Cross

Lythe and listin, gentilmen,
That be of frebore blode;
I shall you tel of a gode yeman,
His name was Robyn Hode.

A Geste of Robyn Hode

Patris sapientia

i, robenhode, englisc of barnysdale,
cattle thief, siccarius, brigand
of the great north road,
from the dungeons of the empyrean
syng the travails of my people.
swindled from blode, exiled
on our own grene earth,
severed the dreaming umbilicus.
a muzzled bear-whelp
with plier-pulled claws, giddy
on the hotplate. stop dancing
and feel the burn.

when brother fights brother,
fellowship fails. tautology
of the weak. tostig's cain-brand,
the oathbreaker dead
and lamech inherits our earth.
gallows seventy times seven:
the bastard's lesson in blood.
a few drew their daggers:
hereward, eadric, wulfric;
but the aetheling spirit bled out
at senlac and stamford bridge.
the ealdormen quit and learned french:
for lords will have their manors.

on the eve of christes mass
1167 joon cyning was whelped
in the palace at oxford
on seventeen silken mattresses,
each one softer than the last.
yet marie, jhesu's modir, leide hym
in a cratche in the shit of beestys.
the spotless shall be praised
and synne's right is nout but work;

adam and his wijf eue, delving
and weaving, not less the cyng
and his quene. *a deo rex, a rege lex?*
ballocks! the law is from god,
and the king is from the people.

ic geseah on swefne a manne
of our cynne, blynded of eie
and lopped of foot, in beggary
at my skel on watlygne street.
and he cwaeth, against the vert
and venison of the french king's
forest have i synned. and then came
a pore mother, meatless ribs
like a flamburgh coble, pot-bellied
manne-whelp gnawing at the tit,
saying, my lord hath brenneth
me out by fire and starved us
from the land; much cattyl is there,
deer and gentil manors,
but the englisc folc no moor.

in my black cloak and black boots
and black witchfinder's hat, i stride
through the mud of the dismantled priory
to the ancient pilgrimmed road,
where thirty thousand with pikes
and rosaries marched under the flag
of the five wounds of christ.
at the whitewashed church
of feastless laurence, bread is just bread
and wine is wine indeed.
candlemas monday, another working day.
the priest would bless the plough
and absolve us from our sinnes.
the saints gave us solace and play.
and what have we now? work
and the word, the interminable pulpit.

in the fiery yeards of myccelgeat,
spinsters slave at flemish looms.
cottars and ploughboys, manacled
to the forge. chynes and pulleys.
ginnes and whirring gears. masters hocked
to caursines, bonds bleeding
from ledgered counting houses.
whorehouse schit-buckets, tipped-out
on plague-pit streets. ratten-raw
lodgings, brayed up in darkness
by coppersmiths' hammers.
work and the grave, urbi et orbis.
at stobbes he rose with the houndis
at daybreak and them watterd
in the wrang-broc, dogges shaking
bowes in the morning sonne-light,
wagtayles peeping and darting for mayflies
from the boulders in the stream.

whatsoever schall it profiteth a man
that he gaineth the earth but loseth
his own land? that his tongue
become the mark of the beest,
that no-one may trade or speek
without it, but his words become
the world's? that hound is put
to cur and terrier to alaunt
so that dogges designed for purpose
are but fit for pore utilitie? *fyrd sceal
ætsomne, tirfæstra getrum*: the people
in the land, knowing they are the people,
knowing it is their land.

forest for deer, covert for fox,
plantation for pheasant and erasing
the hovels of the poor. moor for grouse,
river for grilse. village for the rich,
farmhouse for the profit: barley, linseed,
oilseed rape; polytunnels, fishing lakes,
off-road muck-tracks, land-fill quarries

and mines. hayfields for corncrakes,
islands for the erne, fenland
for spoonbill and crane. the people
in their high estates look down:
on the pinks of the belvoir,
the national trust, the fleeces and gaiters
of the rspb. KEEP OUT.

i saw in a dream the fluoroxypyr
wheatfield bridal with hawthorns,
sown in the shite of winter fieldfares.
men there: walking dogs, picking bluestalks,
releasing pigs to pannage. ergot
on rye, the dried-fumes of harvest mice.
bread in burning vision. the field-stone
foundations of barns and homesteads.
horses in the hay-cut; sweet vernal,
fescue, yorkshire fog: and in the smoking dawn,
walking hares up to the slip, a line of figures
from the luttrell psalter, treading the earth
of the hundred acre wheatfield.

>   *an aungel of the lord came to me in sleep*
>   *and cwaeth, rise noble robenhode*
>   *and slay the frenchman's shire reeve:*
>   *john ball's absolution awaits thee.*
>
>   *john litel and scathelock slew him in saylis*
>   *and stuffed his corps in a broc-hole at smeeton.*
>
>   *the tithe of the lord was death*
>   *and at sword-edge was servitude ended.*
>
>   *and again he cwaeth, may the many-manored*
>   *dukes and mansioned marquesses*
>   *be abdicate and appropriated. and we dwelt*
>   *on the land like the israelites in tents,*
>   *bylding our covenant from the wild stones*
>   *of the feeld, feeding our earth with much blood.*

46

Hours of the Holy Spirit

'1:1 And whanne the daies of Pentecost weren fillid,
alles the disciplis were togidre in the same place.
1:2 And soydennli ther was maad a sown fro heuene,
as of a greet wynde comynge, and it fillide al the hous
where thei saten. 1:3 And diuerse tungis as fier apperiden
to hem, and it sat on ech of hem. 1:4 And all weren fillid
with the Hooli Goost …'

Acts of the Apostles

> *Johon Schepe, som tyme Seynte Marie*
> *prest of York, gretyh you wele alle*
>
> *and doth yowe to understande*
> *he hath rungen youre belle. Stondeth togidre*
>
> *in Godes name; Peres Ploughman,*
> *go to his werk and chastise wel*
> *Hobbe the Robbere: be war ye, or be wo.*

Note well our trueman Cyril Atkinson
who defied Norwood's shotgun
and Rooke's barbed wire to walk Barnsdale's
dirt-roads open for the people.

And our brother Aaron Wilkinson,
who from our own spilled blood and expropriate
soil, wrote his History of South Kirkby
in priceless Silvine notebooks.

Billy Whitehurst of Hickleton Main
who terrorized Hansen and the Daily Mail
with elbows, head-butts and bare-knuckle
bar fights, for the greater glory of Thurnsca.

John Johnson of York, who sought to kill
the scotch king, and who 'kept his crosses
and idle ceremonies' to the death,
honouring the Virgin, giving no quarter.

Hatfield's Dave Douglass – red-ragger, siccarius,
man of rough letters, anarcho-syndicalist,
hewer of coal – who would yet destroy the lords
of this realm, their cops and judges and lawyers.

Brian Plummer, the sainted patron
of Harlington maggot farm, entering the dumps
of coal-soiled cities, finding truth in rat-holes,
the pits of conies, Charlie's reeking earth.

And Ponty's John Nevison, hanged
at Clifford's Tower, committed to Our Lady's earth
under Castlegate's dreaming spire:
unmourned, unmarked: never to be forgotten.

> *With fyre and stave and Wycliffe's worde*
> *wil the commons com into their Kyngdom.*
>
> *The king's corps nailed to the walls*
> *of Beth Shean, dogges licking up the blode.*
>
> *I, Johon Schepe, ministereth to my floc,*
> *and quoth: blessed be the pore, for Englaland*
> *is herne; thei schulen welde the erthe.*

Septem psalmi paenitentiales

'Purge me with hyssope and I shalbe cleane:
wash me, and I shall be whiter then snow.'

Psal LI: 7

Domine, ne in furore

John Nevison makes confession to the priest
at St. Marychurch, Rotherhithe

Shut up and listen. I killed
a horse. I led it to the river
and cut its throat. She was
a good horse, my Father's.
I knew her all my life.
But I thought they might trace me
through her – you know,
at the inn? I had to get rid,
so I killed her. Why didn't I
just cut her loose on the common?
I wasn't thinking straight,
knowing the law would soon
be on my trail. Ten pounds
and a set of silver spoons.
That should see me right
for a few weeks, until I get
settled. The old man'll
be alright. There's plenty more
where that came from.
I get bored, need some action!
Reinvent myself down here.
That poor horse. Lord,
rebuke me not in thine
anger. Blessed Mary,
ever virgin, pray for me.

Beati, quorum remissae

*John Nevison makes confession to the priest
at L'Eglise Ste. Eloi, Dunkerque*

She was no doxy. A rich kid
hot for adventure, that's all,
fresh-fruit, ripe and ready
for plucking by an unprincipled
scrumper like me. I picked her up
in Sint Pieterskerk, on the feast
Our Lady's Visitation. I'd swiped
two-hundred from the Smoke
and was wearing most of it.
I looked good and she knew it.
That night she brought her
Father's wallet and I took
her cherry. The door came in
that morning, flemish burghers
with clubs and muskets:
her to the convent, me to the gaol.
We broke out together and met
at an inn on Visserkaal.
When I lifted her skirts,
she was pussy with the pox.
A purse of silver and a street
of Spanish whores;
not a good combination
for a northern rube like me.
Anyway, to cut a long story short,
I left her sobbing in the street
and signed up with Don John,
which brings me here today.
When I think of her, I think
of Our Lady. Blessed
is he whose transgression
is forgiven. By God's grace
and the intercession
of the Virgin, I will sin no more.

Domine, ne in furore

John Nevison makes confession to the priest
at St. Mary Magdalene, Smeaton

Forgive me Father,
for I have sinned;
An old bloke with a lad
and a hundred geese,
driving to Danum
on the Great North Road.
I had to tithe him; it's what
I do. But there were four of us,
and I owed at Wentbridge
for board and dodge. Plus,
Brace knew a fellow at Pomfret
who would give him good price
for geslin or swan. He should've
just let us take them, but he was set
on being be a hero. We left him
bloody in the ditch at Scawsby,
lad legging it over the moor.
When it came up in the White Hart,
at Elmsall, I denied it was me,
and they were eager to believe it:
round here I'm Robin Hood;
you know, robbing the rich,
if not giving much to the poor.
It's one of the reasons nobody narks.
Anyway, I'm not proud of it;
we should've waited
for your Bishop and done him
at the Skel. Lord, rebuke me
not in thy wrath, nor chasten
me in thy hot displeasure.
I have declared my iniquity
and am sorry for my sin.

Miserere mei

*John Nevison makes confession to the priest
at St. Mary Magdalene, Smeaton*

You never thought you'd hear
from me again, did you?
Well, I bust out of that Moroccan
hell-hole no problem.
It's all backsheesh over there,
and I had thirty gold angels
stitched into my coat and breeches.
That got me to the docks
in a dungcart and passage
to Marseille in a hold of stinking
goatskins. From there I bought
a horse and made my own way
North. But that's not why
I'm here. The plague hit overnight.
The moors were dropping like flies
and the dark hold of the argosy
was murmuring around me.
I broke cover to inform the captain,
a Venetian from Genoa.
He hauled out two lads at flintlock-point.
They kneeled trembling in the sun,
basted in their own sweat,
blotchy as sheepdogs. One was
the baksheesh boy that helped me.
The captain handed me the flintlocks
with a look, as if it was my fault.
I saw how it could go, and I did
what I had to do. They gaffed
them off the side like tunny.
Me, I was checking myself
for buboes all the way to Boulogne.
Have mercy on me, O God,
for I was conceived in sin
and my iniquity is always before me.

Domini exaudi orationem

John Nevison makes confession to the priest
at St. Mary Magdalene, Smeaton

Father, I'm sorry you have
to hear this. I robbed some duke
at Wentbridge and the militia
were on my tail. So I ran to earth
at this inn at Brierley Gap.
John Johnson was my name
to any who asked. I was there
three weeks, my feet well and truly
under the table. I won more
at dice than I did on the Toby.
Hawkesworth, the innkeep,
looked after me noble, with beef
and beer and tipping me the wink.
I tried to do right by him; I kept
a low profile and made sure
swag found its way to his door,
even as his woman was finding her way
to mine. She was a gleeting slut,
but even so: that's how I repaid him.
The heat died down. I got bored
and readied to bail. She'd packed her bags.
She thought I was taking her with me.
I put her right with a slap
and told her to button it.
Hawkesworth shook my hand
and bid me return. Sometimes
I wish I was a clerk or a cowman.
Hear, O Lord, my prayer.

De profundis

John Nevison makes confession to the priest
at St. Helen's, Sandal Magna.

I killed a bounty hunter
named Darcy Fletcher.
Him and his brother got a tip
from a nark and came to arrest me
at the Needless Inn at Howley.
They caught me cold,
hungover in bed with some scrubber.
I woke to cocked-pistols
pointing at my head, shiny grinning faces.
I had two loaded flintlocks
under the blankets and I fired them both.
The bed set on fire; I was jumping
about bollock-naked like a twat.
One went down with a hole in his head,
the other clattered screaming down the stairs.
I think I winged him. And all
for twenty quid. I'd pissed that
up the wall in the bar the night before.
Anyway, I tossed the tart a shilling
and ran. Behind me, that damned nark inn
burned down. I don't know why
I'm telling you this: I'm not sorry.
My only regret is I didn't finish
the brother. Out of the depths, Lord.
Lady, be attentive to the voice
of my supplications.

Domini exaudi orationem

*John Nevison addresses his people after
making confession to the priest at St. Mary
Magdalene, Castlegate, York.*

Where do I start?   I'm a thief, a cheat,
a con-man and killer, a drunk
and a whoremonger. What else?
A footpad and forger,
every now and then a traitor;
but mostly - just scum.
I've confessed it all and received
absolution; I go to the gallows
in good cheer, confident
of the life eternal; if not
in Elysium, then in the memory
of the people, their ballads
and bar room tales - I'd get in the beer,
toss pennies for their children,
shoot it out with the militia.
Plus, I gave the toffs hell.
They loved that best, and so did I.
I had a good run. So let's get it done:
strap me to a hurdle and drag me
to the Knavesmire.   Brace and Tankard
will avenge my death; they'll dangle
the nark from the Judas tree
and open Hardcastle's throat.
Hear my prayer O Lord - cut off
mine enemies and destroy all them
that afflict the soul of the people.
God save the King and his commons!

Hours of the Dead

*'Who are the dead? Who are the living
and the dead?'*

Allen Tate, *The Oath*

John Schepe at the altar of St. Leonard's Church
in the butterfly wood at Tinsley.

A child in the graveyard pulling femurs
from the earth; Mortain and Maerleswin,
the rickety pins of serfs. Turf tumescent
and studded with daisies, rooting from the dead.
Headstones rotting under bowed laburnums,
the riven sandstone sundial. Surnames
in copperplate; Atte-Hall, Stillingfleet, Warde.
A clambering idiot, smearing mistletoe
on poplars, stealing seeds from the hoary crabtree.
Tractor on the low road. Gravel-crunching Mercs.
Owl pellets and stale confetti. The packed-lunch
vista over Mappleyard to Frickley,
examining our treasure: a bag of old bones,
decades of flaccid bellis perennis,
the star-pipped flesh of crabs.

*Bread and cheese, small beer; the mad cantor's
levelling stipend, worthy to receive.*

Under the golf course, the dead of England lie;
beneath the steel mill, their vernacular graves.
Rolling and turning in tectonic earth,
drifting turfward in turbulent methane,
the sphenoids of huscarls reveal in the borders
of the Whitehill Estate. Traffic roar
and HiViz jackets. Suits, ties and shiny shoes.
Ant and Dec, Summertime Special,
seventy two bottles of Bud. Grylls, Mears
and Whittingstall, their fossil-fuel junkets,
screaming through the wildwood. XR3i,
parked outside the Goldmine, hi-NRG's
octave bassline shaking down the walls.
Jase Burt, Neil Grose, Ian Scrivens,
zipped into body-bags on the scoured slopes
of Longden. And the Funboy Three
in Sol's Market Fisheries, singing to the tune
of the drunken sailor: *What shall we do
with the Argentinians, erlie in the morning?
Bomb, bomb, bomb the bastards …*

Athelstan's guilt offering, for Earls and Kings,
his own unsainted soul. For the blood of Christ
was insufficient on Weondune's hazelled field.

Whit picnic at the Sheepwash, damp-arsed
among kingcups and yorkshire fog,
chomping bread and jam. Who's a Bobby Dazzler
in two quid sneakers fresh from Bernard Miller's?
Me, cupping my hand in the bullhead stream,
slurping from the flow like a dirty bugger.
The arable water tasted like muck
and organophosphates. A Wimpey's expedition;
me, Gaz, Beaver and Millsy, half-way
between Kirkby and Hemsworth, where
the farmers of Limphill and Hague Hall farms
used to dip their sheep in the stream. It's not
on any maps, but one sweltering Sunday
in the miners' strike, Arthur Wakefield
stopped there to thumb a lift to the Alpha.
It's where Flick Spencer used to watter his dogs,
Michelle Appleyard her horse. Stu Priestley raced
Ness there and back from Buck's Farm,
and Crazy Horse Hampton lost it on the curve,
flinging Millsy face first from his helmetless
pillion, into the sodium lamp-post:
broken in the silts of the funerary waters.

Sometimes the sword. For John Schepe's floc
is fled to the ravenings of wolfish men.
Middle-earth shrunk to food and devouring:
past and future – silent birthblind dreams.

Transitions of the Virgin in Hampole Wood:
milky galanthus and snowbright anemones
drifting under bare-bone oaks; equinoctal
narcissi, funnelling the sun; sky-belled
hyacinthus. The immemorial robings
of Barnsdale, unwitnessed by Richard Rolle,
graved under the Aga in Abbey House;
George Speight, the long-gone forester,
birches sprouting from his roofless-hearth,
dormice dozing in the derelict coppice;
the dissolute heirs of Rat Hall Farm,
their insolent gibbet of corvids.
Roe kids suckling at the fork to Lound Lane,
amid mounds of fly-tipped builders' rubble;
where we rediscovered harebells and quaking grass,
were savaged by Rat Hall's German Shepherds
and where they plucked out the stump
of the pilgrim waycross with the front bucket of a JCB.

John Schepe to his floc from the steps of St. Laurence
in Tinsley's fallen wood: resurrect the mute dead
from their amnesiac graves, rewrite their trivia
on memory's scraped-off page.

What is that bird calling from the dusk?
Spiritous mists are chilling the outside air.
Close the window. There again through the glass:
a mournful puit, a curlew's severed plaint,
a loon's sinister atmospherics
at Camp Crystal Lake. Turn off the light.
Sit in silence by the window and listen
through the stare of your black doppelganger,
as springtide darkness presses against the glaze.
A blackbird's alarums, the frantic ticking of robins -
cat-yowl, maybe, clawed-paws flipping the lid
of the tit-box? Sally forth in carpet slippers,
brandishing yard-brush. Blackbirds and robins erupt -
and haloed in the moon on the herringbone aerial:
athene noctua, presaging death in this suburb.
These ghosts are drawn by my own fuming blood.

To hedgerow crones, pulling the screaming mandrake,
bloodwine and breadbody John Schepe brings.
For God made for you herb and unguent brockfat
and stowed them in our apotek woods.

When we tipped out his ashes, some fell
on our shoes. We scraped them clean
in the heather. Nobody knew what to say;
we filled up and stammered. And that was it.
We made a walk of it and stopped off
for fish and chips on the way home.
The following year, I drove up there
with a sapling yew and planted it at the spot.
It ought to be as tall as a man by now,
but sheep and rabbits have gnawed it
to a stick. I visit once or twice a year,
say some words, then make a walk of it.
Is that what he wanted? Why not his name
on a marble slab in the native soil
of our Carr Lane cemetery? *In memory*
of Clarence Ely, 1940-2002. We could've
gone there every week, kids and grandkids,
with flowers and knick-knacks, melancholy
bullshit and laughing out loud. But that ship
has sailed. So all our love, Dad, in your exile
on Horcum, there unmourned by the lonely
curlew, on the bee-less purple moor.

John Schepe from the scaffold to Eden's fieldfolc:
birdlime, ploughs and snares. Beer and bread.
One Holy Catholick and Apostolic Church
hallowing the life and times of the people.

In the cabaret at Strytem, pronouncing the beer
like cowshit, wheeler William Rockliff,
driver James Crammond and gunner John Butterworth
of the Royal Horse Artillery got royal for tuppence
on flemish gin. The frogs in the moat
around their billet kept them from sleep
with their damnable croaking. So Rockliff
made a raft, and arming themselves with clubs,
they sailed forth that midnight to bash out their brains.
At dawn the boot-and-saddle sounded, calling them
to the front, bleary and stinking like otters;
where Crammond's head was shattered by grapeshot,
and Butterworth blown to pieces by his own cannon.
William Rockliff, veteran of Seringapatam
and Salamanca, survived to bodge chairs
in the officer's mess at Clichy, a pause
on the march on Paris. He returned home
to Ned Ludd and Captain Swing, and a job for life
at Stapleton Park, where he died at the lathe
aged eighty eight. Campaign medal pinned to his chest,
he was buried by his kin in St. Mary's earth
at Smeaton, a hero of Waterloo.

John Schepe's head on a spike at Micklegate Bar,
dribbling maggots, preaching yet.

In my nihilism and solipsism and bravura
low esteem, I told them, throw my corpse
over the back wall for the dogs and magpies.
No church or memorial, just nettles
growing lush through the bleached bones of my ribcage
in a ditch of garden rubbish; I sneaked in
through the back door unnoticed, and I'll leave
the same way; a nothing of life to be matched
by a nothing of death. The workers have no country,
no bloodline to their people or their past.
A starveling present and a cockaigne future:
you only live once! But I'm a changed man
in my people and my land. Heaven or hell
will do what they will. I've lived my life
and confessed my sins. So bury me in our earth
at the plague church at Frickley, east of the gate,
south of the gas gun, under the Virgin's
dessicate hawthorns. Like Depledge and Speight,
Rockliff and Jennings, my stone will tell my story.

Scarlok and the miller's son, lurking by the Skel
on Watlynge Street, clutching their daggers.

Memorials of the Saints

'...homines indomabiles et durae ac barbarae mentis...'

Bede, *Ecclesiastical History* III:5

Arthur Scargill

The lowest of the low and low-paid,
the primary men; farmhands, quarrymen, *colliers*.
Crude men, of appetite and violence, mumblers,
white-knucklers, averters of eyes. Beasts of burden,
their lives lived out in the rhythm
of the Coal Board's seasons: days and afters,
Henry Halls, neets reg. Larks orbiting the wheel
and the cold cage falling. Crushed torsos under splintered
chocks, amputations on the maingate rip,
blood-streaked phlegm hocked-up. Surface to the land
of cockaigne: egg and chips, beer and the bookies.
You brought them health and Palma de Mallorca,
Cortinas on the drive and kids in college,
reading Marx and Mao and *The Wealth of Nations*.

Wayne Johnson

He'll see you in the tunnel or the car park.
Your orbital sockets will crack like wood,
you'll be spitting out teeth like tic-tacs.
Get ready for his bite in the gristle of your ear,
his chawing in the cartilage of your nose.
He's a good lad though: shake hands mate?
Two gallon in the club and a thousand stories:
sparked out pikeys, shit-scared half-backs,
turds floating in the bath; swung elbows
and cracked patellas, greensticked tib and fib.
Careful what you say, though, because he'll flip
like that; he'll do you in the bogs or outside
the fish shop, leave you paramedicked
in the street. Are we glad he's on our side!

Dismas, the good thief

Compassion, fear of Judgement,
acknowledgement of transgression, acceptance
of earthly justice, implicit repentance,
faith. All in four verses. Christ himself
gave absolution, and why wouldn't he?
He ticked all the boxes. The nails still drove in,
and they had to, being the just sentence
for his crimes; the alternative being
social work and poor-you counselling
from the Howard League for Penal Reform.
But for the serial thefts from ASDA
and Weavers, the Allied Supplies break-ins,
the gang-assaults, arsons, recreation ground rapes:
today shalt thou be with me in Paradise.

John Ball

Wycliffe's words and Langland's gave the Englisc
back their tongue. Manor french and church latin,
cut-off in the throat, battening behind
the buttresses of keeps and cathedrals,
parsing and declining. Johon Schepe
proclaims his hedgerow gospel, singing
from the furze like a yellowhammer:
Johan the Mullere hath ygrounde smal, smal, smal.
The Kynges sone of hevene schal pay for al.
Be war or ye be wo; Knoweth your freend
fro your foo. Haveth ynow, and seith 'Hoo!'
There were no lords in Eden's commune.
Scythes sharpened on whetstones, *gente non sancta.*
War will follow the Word.

John Nevison

Eddie McGee tracked you from Wentbridge to Malton
by the way your horse shit on the highway.
Bent over with his magnifying glass,
sniffing at the fumes, standing up and pointing –
he went that-a-way! You sold that horse
at Driffield and took a coach to Hull,
where you bummed a ride on a hoecker
to Lynn, taking five hundred gold marks
from a merchant of the Hansa, giving the money
to a widow, or founding a church. You was always
a gennelman. Meanwhile, old Eddie
was kicking down doors at the tennis courts
at Malton, having traced your DNA through the dew.
Barry Prudom is my friend, he kills coppers.

Joseph the Dreamer

A beard for the Virgin, genealogically
correct, with a trade to support his wife
and God's kid. Joseph the joiner,
line of David, husband of Mary,
the bland paternal surrogate of our Lord;
written out of the script by chapter three.
But like his namesake, also a dreamer,
hard-wired in biddance to the Angel
of the Lord. He dreamed, and it was done:
hineniy, Adonai, hineniy. In and out of Egypt
in accordance with the scriptures,
leading his people to a land of new promise,
via Galilee of the gentiles
and thereon to Jerusalem and the world.

Michael the Archangel

Little John's Well at Stubbs dried up
as limestone quarrying behind the scarp
progressively destroyed the water table.
Dry years, as earth-locked rain burrowed
and bored in the bones of Barnsdale, before breaking
to the light in a winter-wheat field,
east of the Ea Beck bridge. Soon, rags were tied
to streamside trees and silver sown
in the muck's bright mirror. An underground
tradition, like midrash or the cult of saints,
bubbling forth like a rolling boil:
one harrowing hell with the corpse
of Moses, under the guns of Randi
and Dawkins, the canons of the Church.

Mary Magdalene

Vain Belias, Carnivean the lewd
and Berith of strife. And four more conjured
from the babbling world or via the Enochian Keys.
A whore, allegedly, replete with vices,
snared in her sordid quotidian –
Closer! Primark, nails and extensions,
Loose Women's eternal hen-night,
the wild-dog savaging of librarians
and nuns. He laid on hands and freed
her from that world: *your sins are forgiven.*
Sudden death falling like a midseason sale;
Rosier preens in grief, shops for roadside flowers:
you witnessing by the ghostless body,
in the slab-cold luminous tomb.

Paul

You were a thorn in everyone's flesh,
for you determined to know nothing
in this world but Christ and him crucified.
The God-fearing goyim of the Roman galut
knelt at his supper, giving thanks
for their foreskins, for pork and prawns
and the life everlasting. Those reputed
to be pillars murmured against you,
spreading slanders in the synagogues.
But you held your line, in tract and epistle
and to Kephas face to face. *Christ and him crucified*,
rain or shine, from Antioch to Cadiz –
with Big Jeff and Gaz Hutsby, shouting *Socialist Worker!*
under the clock at South Elmsall Market.

Richard Rolle

Deep Dale, set back from the high road,
a cell of wildwood stone. Lenten sunlight
squinting through oak boughs, dappling shadow.
Grass snakes unfurling from last year's bracken,
frayed heads of narcissi gone over;
stitchwort and bluebell, yellow archangel,
now coming into their kingdom.
On the earth path from Hampole
comes big-bosomed Margret, bearing bread, beer
and shitbucket. Gledes mewing overhead.
Willow-wren tight in her feathery cave.
Dwale in the leaf litter, a woodcock's liquid eye.
And ringing through Barnsdale's sultry forest,
the nightingale's hot sweet song.

Robert Aske

Cinquefoil and creeping tormentil
watered in the wine of five rivers struck
from the bread of his temple: Derwent, Aire,
Went, Ea and Skell. Heavy horse and hobnails,
tramping over bridges, camped under banners
at Cheswold's starry gate. Pierced by blades,
blood and water came forth; his lopped head
rolled like a cannonball. They flew him
like a flag from the walls of Clifford's Tower
and scattered his bones for the kites,
swarming over stones at Hampole and Roche,
packing ox-carts with pewter and plate.
Skipper's gold on five-leaf grass, All Saints
graveyard, Aughton: *oblier ne doy.*

Robenhode

Death by venesection. She dosed you
with feverfew then cut across the cords.
Chamomile kept it flowing, first the thick blood,
then the thin. In the dark before dawn
your breathing grew shallow and rattled
in your throat, as you whispered your houzle
into John Little's ear, him raging to fire
and sword. In Mary's name, you stayed his hand,
bade him help you bend the bow.
You bled out by cock-crow, your lard-white,
unsumped body crimsoning Roger's couch.
The arrow earthed in Barnsdale, and water
came forth. There drinks the fox from his own
cupped hand, under the keeper's gun.

Oswald

At the appointed time, the chief men
of each parish rode Caesar's streets
to assemble at Pomfret's thyng.
From Castleford, Kirkby, eremitic Wragby
and a dozen others. Around your market-rood,
blurred by metathesis – *Osgoldcross* –
the jeers and raised voices of the open air witan,
overlooked by the Old Town Hall.
Today we dream by Giles the hermit,
buying rhubarb and spanish and Reebok Classics,
steak slices from Greggs and SIM-less phones;
glassing each other on the Red Lion's carpets,
or keeping the faith at the Northern Soul night
at the Ancient Borough Arms.

Afterwords

Book of Hours

In the mediaeval period, wealthy pious who wished to pray the Divine Office commissioned their own personal 'Books of Hours'. Often exquisitely illustrated, these books contained a range of devotions – prayers, psalms, antiphons, texts from the Old and New Testaments and so on – to be prayed or sung at the canonical *hours*: matins, lauds, prime, tierce, sext, none, vespers and compline.

Oswald

King of Northumbria, evangelist, martyr and saint. Born in 605, probably at York, Oswald was the first English king to fight under a Christian standard: prior to the battle of Heavenfield in 635, he rallied his fyrd around an improvised wooden cross, going on to win a miraculous victory against the vastly superior forces of the British king Cadwallon, in the process reuniting the hitherto divided kingdom of Northumbria.

Subsequently, Oswald extended his influence far beyond Northumbria. To the south, he frustrated the territorial ambitions of Penda, the pagan English king of Mercia, and those of Cadwalla, successor to Cadwallon. To the north, Oswald dominated the Picts, Scots and the British kingdom of Strathclyde. Oswald's influence grew to the extent he was referred to as 'Bretwalda' – ruler of all Britain.

Oswald spent much of his youth in exile at St. Columba's monastery at Hii (Iona), where his religious beliefs were formed and where he became fluent in Scots (Gaelic). On accession to the throne, he recruited St. Aidan from Hii to evangelise the Northumbrians. Oswald took an active role in this process, often acting as Aidan's interpreter.

On 5 August, 642, Oswald was killed in battle at Maserfield, Shropshire, deep in the territory of his formidable rival, Penda. In a show of pagan contempt, Penda mutilated Oswald's body and displayed his corpse for a full year before Oswald's brother, Oswy, was able to defeat Penda and regain his brother's bones. Elevated to sainthood by popular acclaim, Oswald's relics were soon in the possession of a range of monasteries and churches – his head is interred at Durham Cathedral to this day.